Gospel Story for Kids
New Testament
Coloring Book Two

New
Growth
Press

www.NewGrowthPress.com

Note to User: Each coloring page number corresponds to the same number lesson in the *Gospel Story Curriculum: Following Jesus in the New Testament* and same number week in *Old Story New: Ten-Minute Devotions to Draw Your Family to God*.

New Growth Press, Greensboro, NC 27404
www.newgrowthpress.com
Copyright © 2013 by New Growth Press
Published 2013.

Cover Design: faceout studio, faceoutstudio.com
Art Direction: Matthew Nowicki
Coloring Sheet Art Work: Ramona Doyle

Printed in the USA

20 19 18 17 16 15 14 13   1 2 3 4 5

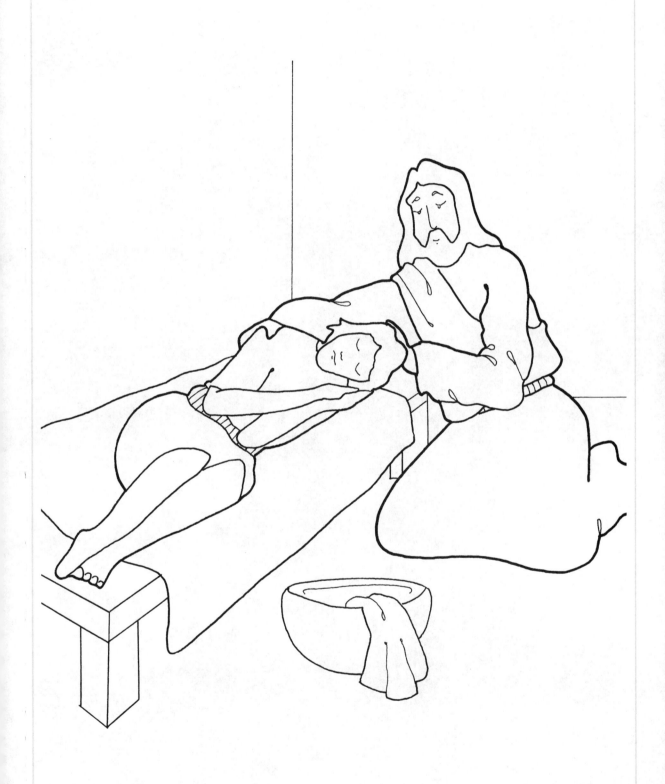

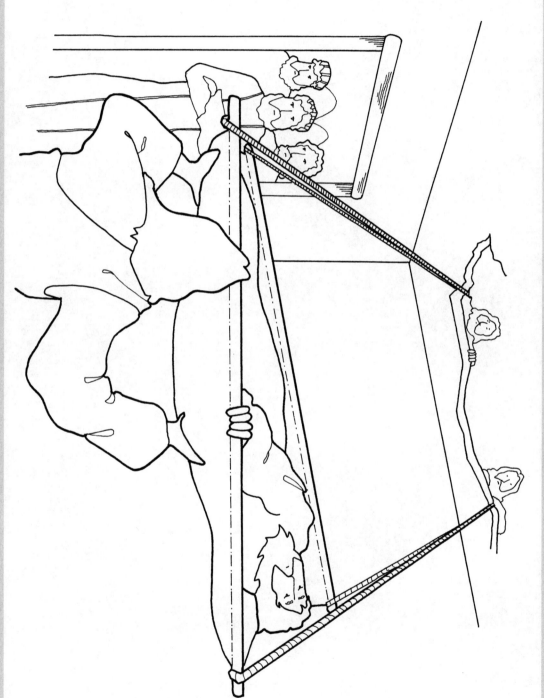

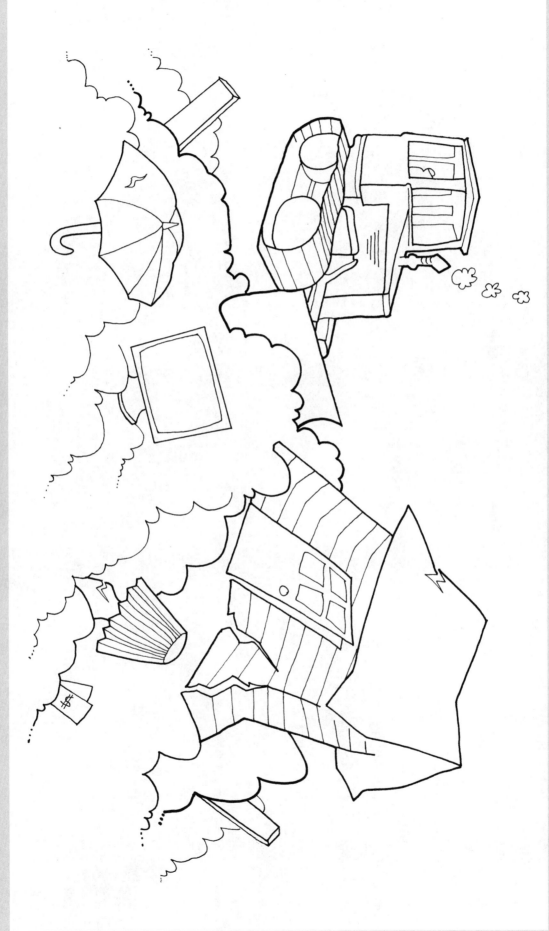

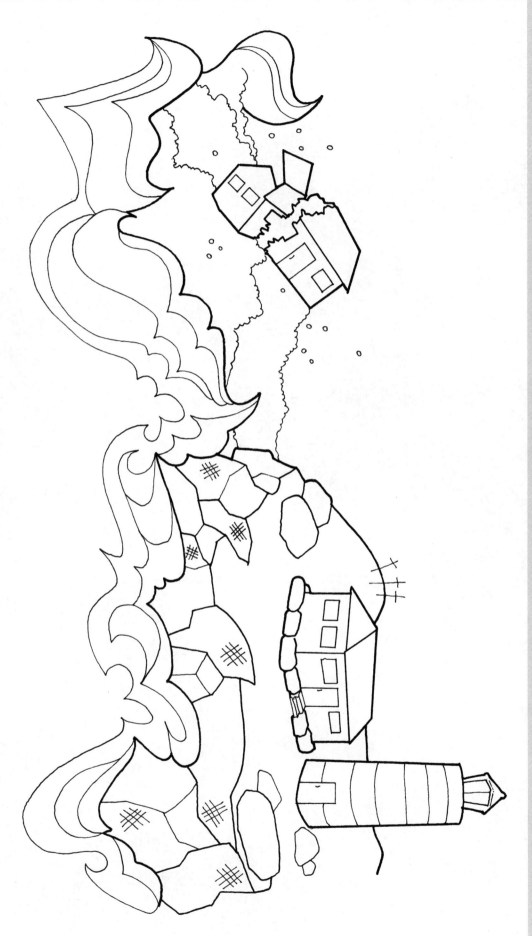

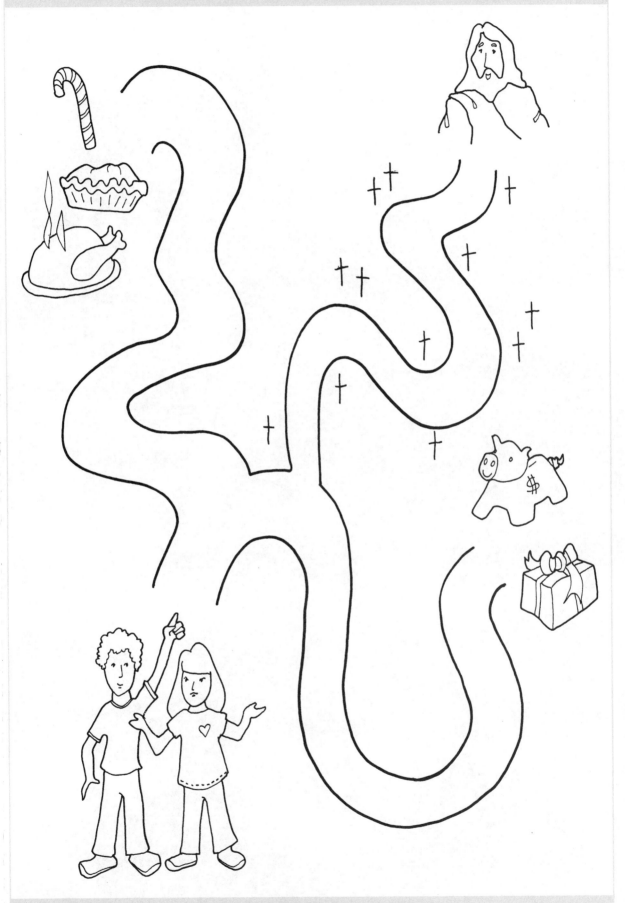

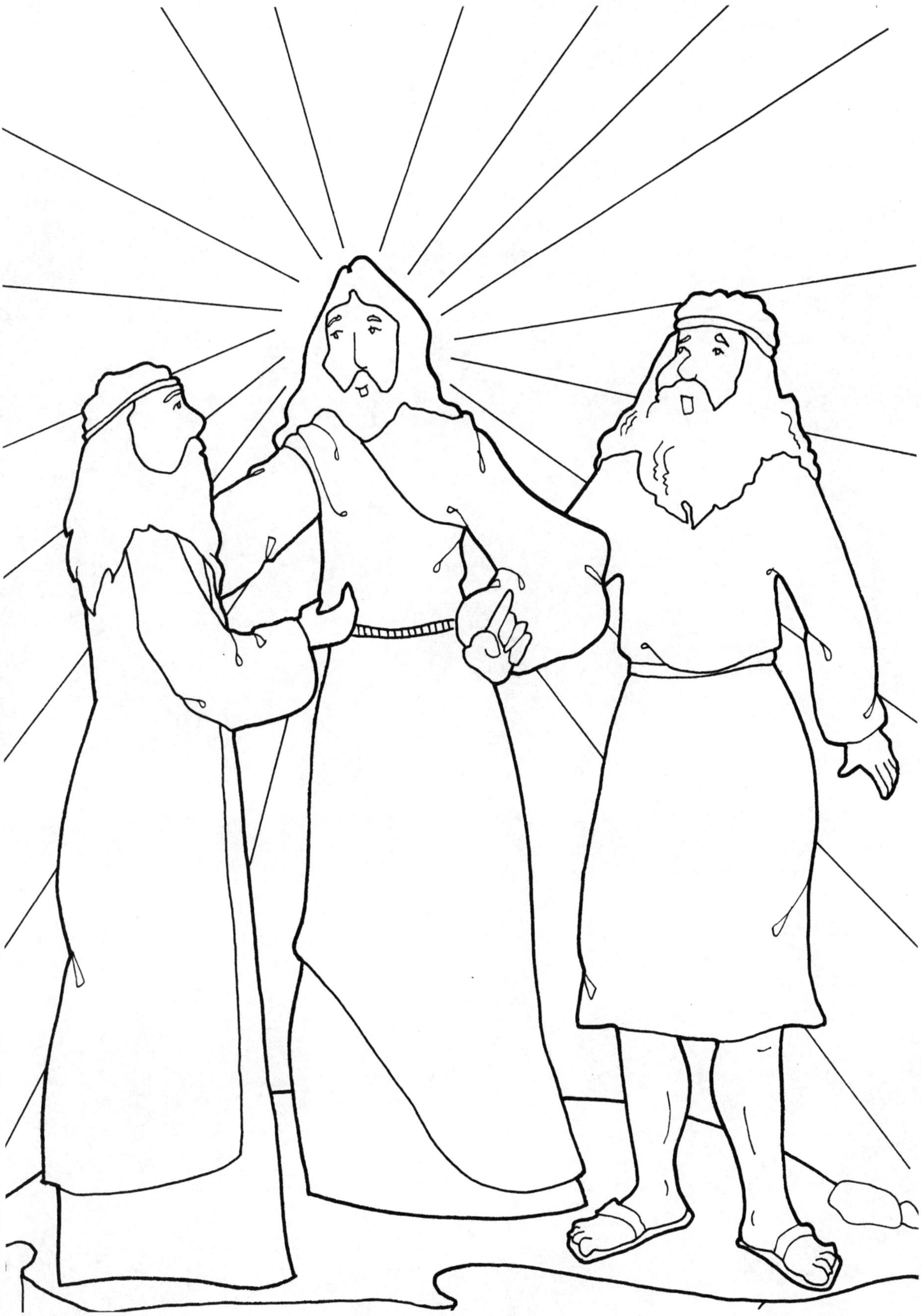

WWW.GOSPELSTORYFORKIDS.COM

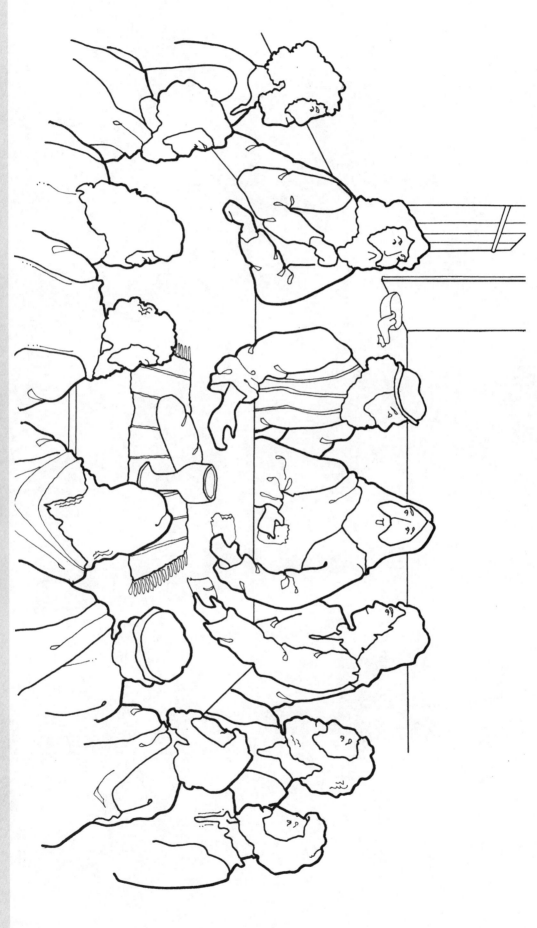

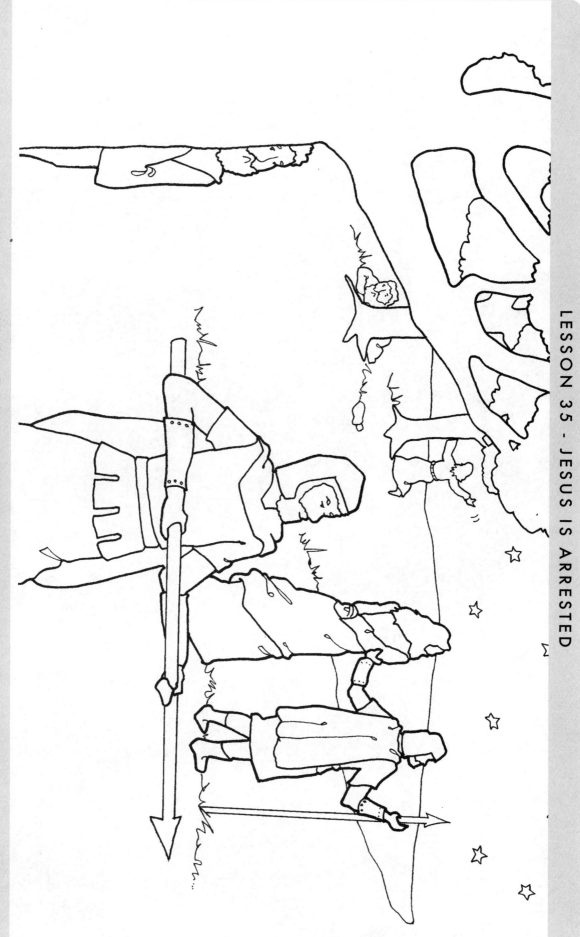

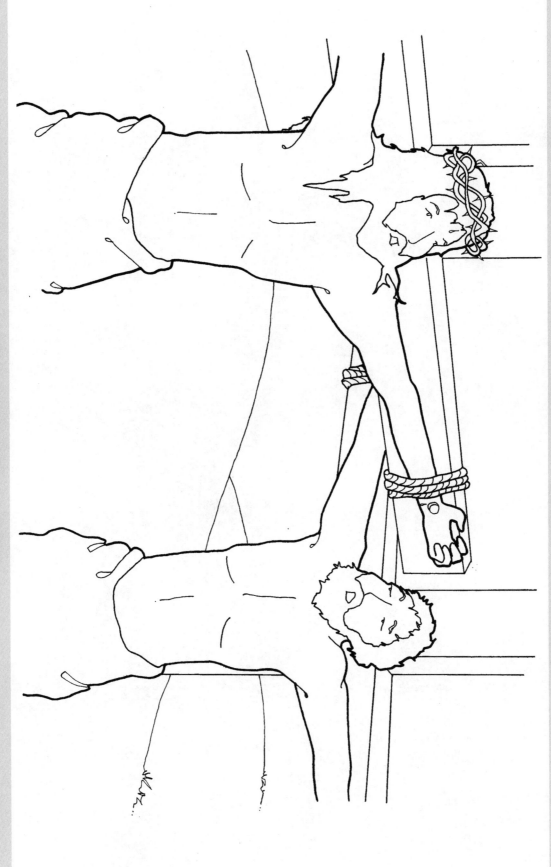

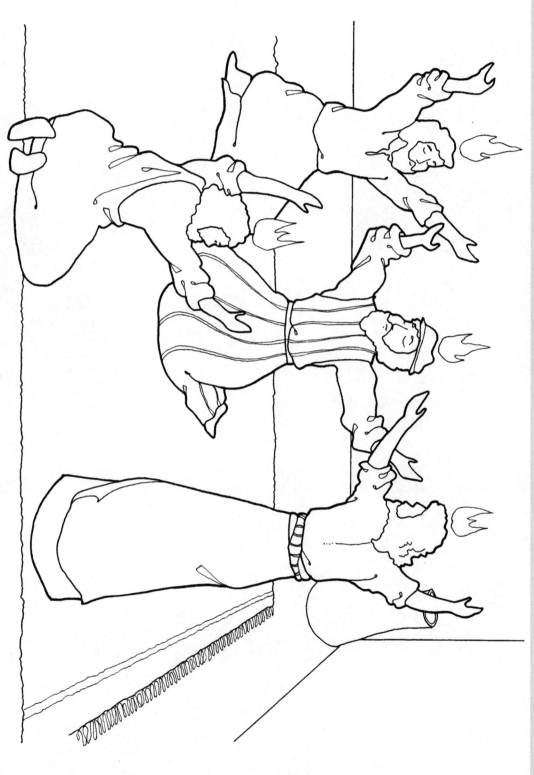

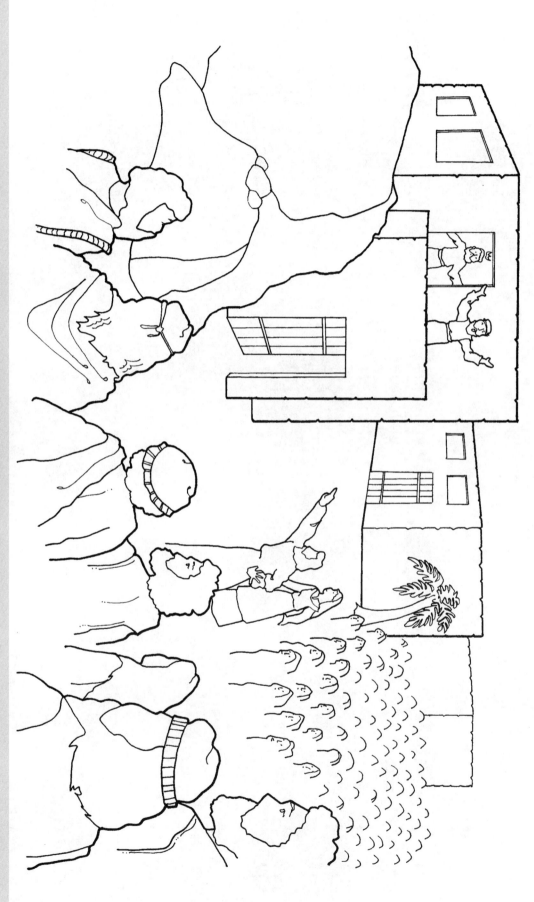

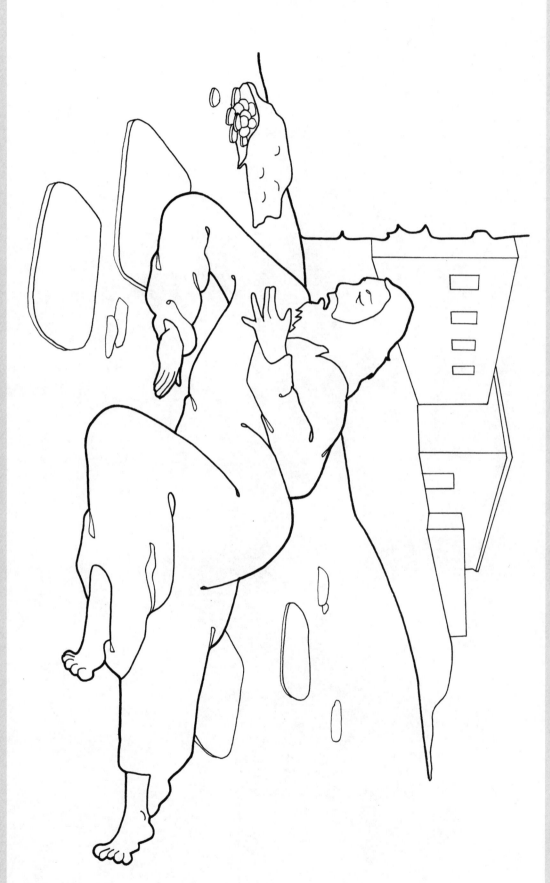

LESSON 48 - ANANIAS & SAPPHIRA

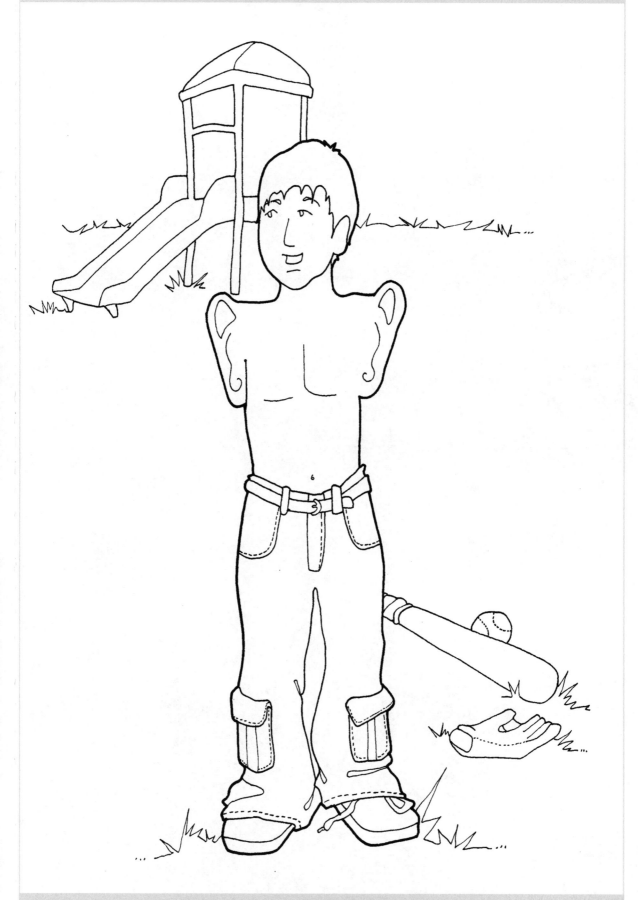

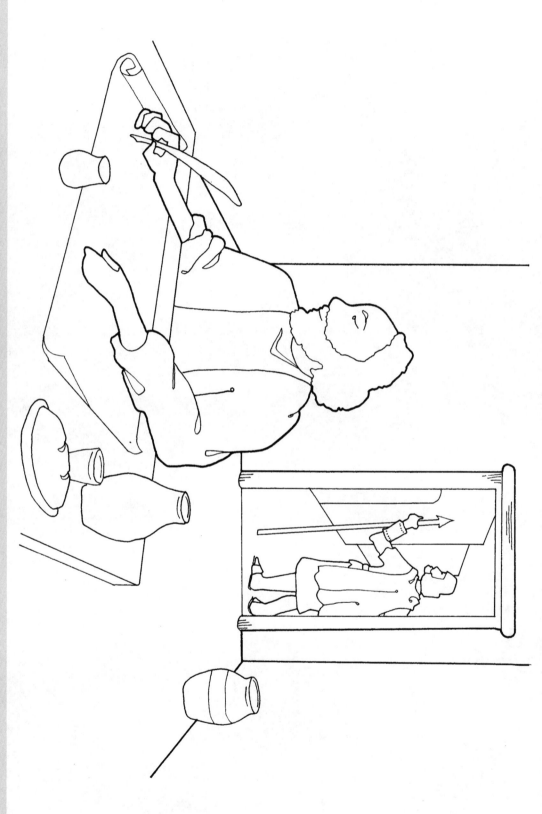

Man looks at the outward appearance but God looks at the heart.

Character Counts!

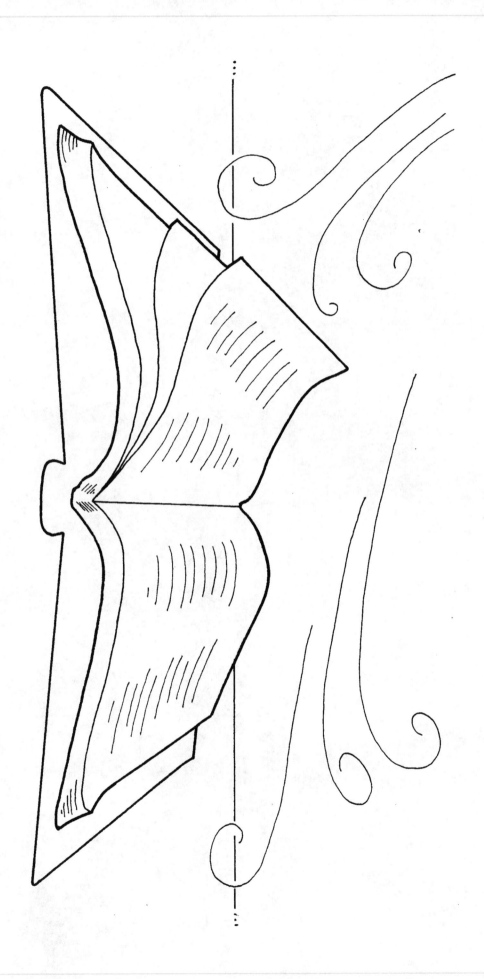

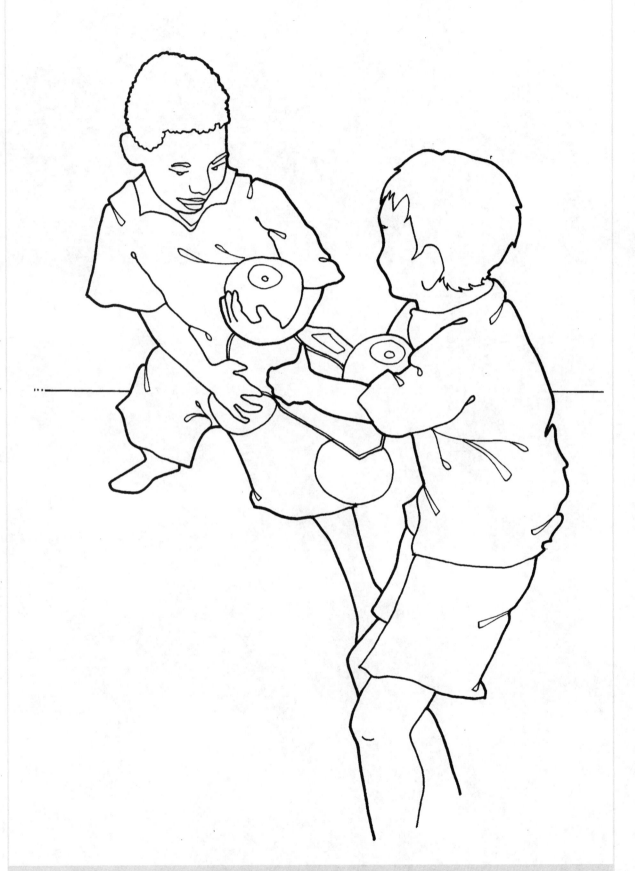

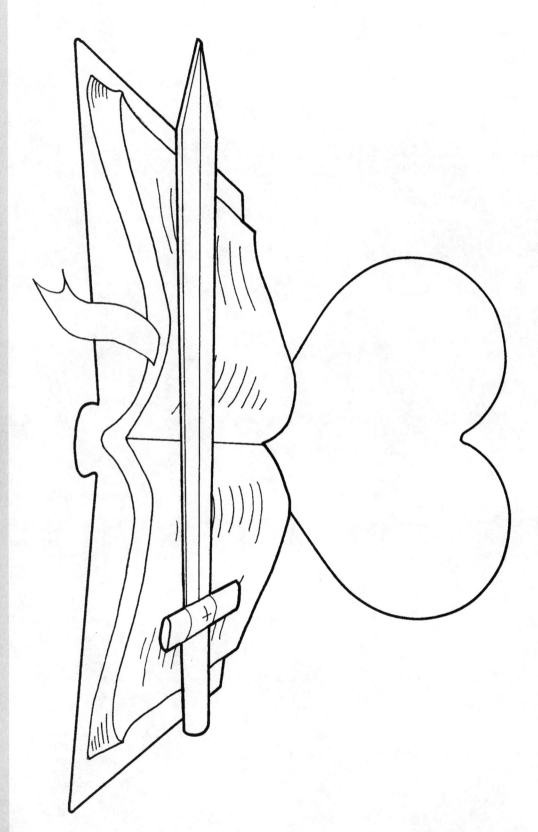

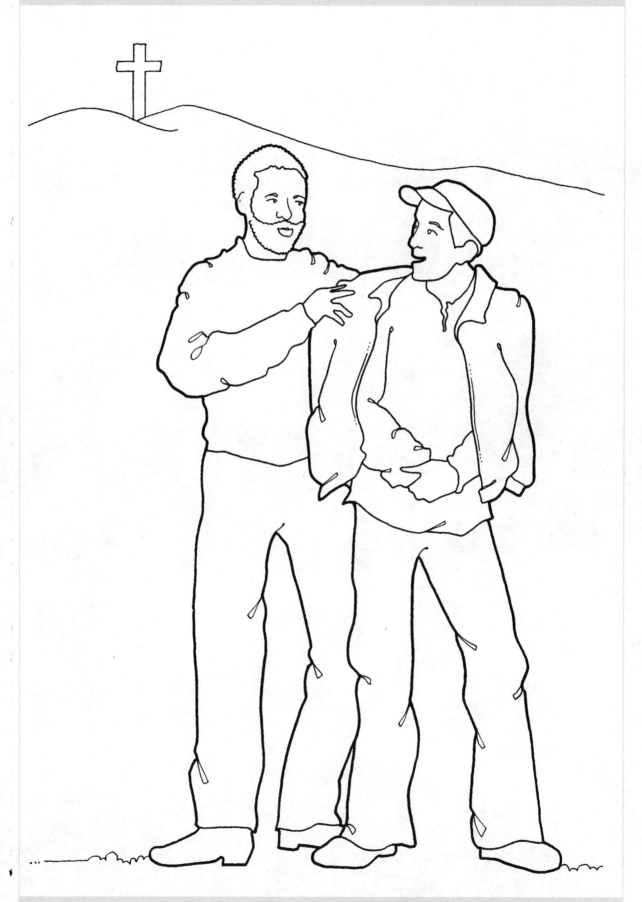

the Gospel Story for Kids

Marty Machowski

A Unique Program Connecting Children to the Gospel Story from Genesis to Revelation

An interactive program for home and classroom that grounds children in gospel-centered, biblical truth. Children who begin this program at age three and continue through age twelve will have absorbed the gospel story from Genesis to Revelation three times. At each age level children are taught the gospel through age-appropriate illustrations, activities, coloring pages, object lessons, and memorization.

Three-year 156 story, Sunday school curriculum for preschool through upper elementary.

Two companion family devotionals, *Long Story Short* (OT) and *Old Story New* (NT) that follow the same 156 stories as the Sunday school curriculum and reinforce the gospel story at home.

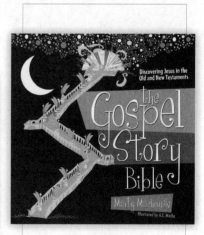

An illustrated Bible storybook, *The Gospel Story Bible*, highlights the same 156 stories for churches and families.